Let's Go! Let's Grow!

WHAT WILL BE BORN?

WILL

Stephanie Anne Box

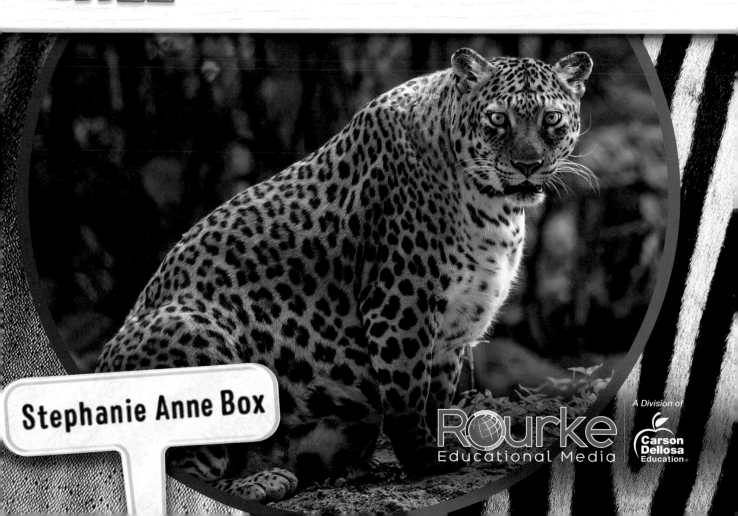

Rourke Educational Media

A Division of Carson Dellosa Education

SCHOOL to HOME
CONNECTIONS
BEFORE AND DURING READING ACTIVITIES

Before Reading: *Building Background Knowledge and Vocabulary*

Building background knowledge can help children process new information and build upon what they already know. Before reading a book, it is important to tap into what children already know about the topic. This will help them develop their vocabulary and increase their reading comprehension.

Questions and Activities to Build Background Knowledge:

1. Look at the front cover of the book and read the title. What do you think this book will be about?
2. What do you already know about this topic?
3. Take a book walk and skim the pages. Look at the table of contents, photographs, captions, and bold words. Did these text features give you any information or predictions about what you will read in this book?

Vocabulary: *Vocabulary Is Key to Reading Comprehension*

Use the following directions to prompt a conversation about each word.
- Read the vocabulary words.
- What comes to mind when you see each word?
- What do you think each word means?

> **Vocabulary Words:**
> - *mammal*
> - *nutrients*
> - *offspring*
> - *pouch*

During Reading: *Reading for Meaning and Understanding*

To achieve deep comprehension of a book, children are encouraged to use close reading strategies. During reading, it is important to have children stop and make connections. These connections result in deeper analysis and understanding of a book.

 Close Reading a Text

During reading, have children stop and talk about the following:
- Any confusing parts
- Any unknown words
- Text to text, text to self, text to world connections
- The main idea in each chapter or heading

Encourage children to use context clues to determine the meaning of any unknown words. These strategies will help children learn to analyze the text more thoroughly as they read.

When you are finished reading this book, turn to the last page for an **After-Reading** activity.

Table of Contents

What Will Be Born?

These **mammals** are going to have babies. What do you think will be born?

Mammals give birth. The babies grow inside their mother. Mammals get **nutrients** from their mother's body.

Mammals have backbones and hair or fur. Most baby mammals look like small forms of their parents.

When some mammals are born, they can survive outside the mother's body. Others are born and continue growing inside the mother's **pouch**.

Did you know some mammals can read? That's right! Humans are mammals, too.

Babies Grow Up

Most mammal babies rely on their mother's milk to live after they are born.

Many mothers stay with their babies.
They take care of them.

They live together for months or years.

Offspring are shown how to find shelter and food. Some mammals look for plants. Some hunt for other animals. Some mammals eat both.

We Are a Family

Many mammals live and hunt in large families. The group takes care of the babies.

Each group of animals has a special name. Did you know a group of giraffes is called a tower?

Many mammals will find a mate. They will have a family of their own. The life cycle repeats.

Look what was born! Did you guess correctly?

Photo Glossary

mammal (MAM-uhl): A warm-blooded animal that has hair or fur and usually gives birth to live babies. Female mammals produce milk to feed their young.

nutrient(s) (NOO-tree-uhnts): A substance such as protein, a mineral, or a vitamin that is needed by people, animals, and plants to stay strong and healthy.

offspring (AWF-spring): The young of an animal or a human being.

pouch (pouch): A pocket in the mother's body in which kangaroos and other marsupials carry their young.

Activity: Make a Mammal Fact Sheet

Think:

You can find mammals everywhere. They live in forests, deserts, oceans, and even the mountains. Think of a time when you have been up close with a mammal.

Supplies

paper
pencil
markers/crayons
computer

Directions:

On a sheet of paper, draw a mammal. What does it look like? Describe where it lives and what it eats. What makes it different than a bird, an amphibian, or a reptile? Write as many details and facts as you can think of. Draw what you think its offspring, or baby, would look like. After you make your fact sheet, do a guided internet search with a parent to learn more.

Index

About the Author

Stephanie Anne Box loves animals and is proud to share her newest book with you. Stephanie is a kindergarten teacher who lives in Mississippi with her husband, Josh, and her dog, Dudley.

After–Reading Activity

Think about the mammals in the book. Imagine being a baby animal, or offspring. See if you can walk like a lion cub, curl up like a joey in a pouch, run like a wolf pup, and gallop like a foal.

Library of Congress PCN Data

What Will Be Born? / Stephanie Anne Box
(Let's Go! Let's Grow!)
ISBN 978-1-73165-177-8 (hard cover)(alk. paper)
ISBN 978-1-73165-222-5 (soft cover)
ISBN 978-1-73165-192-1 (e-Book)
Library of Congress Control Number: 2021944771

Rourke Educational Media
Printed in the United States of America
01-3402111937

Edited by: Laura Malay
Cover design by: Tammy Ortner
Interior design by: Tammy Ortner
Photo Credits: Photo Credits: Cover p 1 © GUILLERMO CERVETTO, © Anna Kucherova, © MaraQu, © NataliaMalc, p 4 © Dolores M. Harvey, p 5 © Matthew Jessop, © Elated Industries, p 6 © David Barlow Photography, p 7 © Daa islam, p 8 © Ewa Studio, © Claudio Bertoloni, © Gerhard Koertner/NHPA/Photoshot/Newscom, p 9 © Syda Productions, p 10 © Juli_li_Photographer, p 11 © frank60, p 12 © agefotostock, p 13 © nwdph, p 14 © Bkamprath, p 15 © Damian Lugowski, p 16 © Nobby Clarke, p 17 © Linda_K, p 18 © SeventyFour, p 19 © P Harstela, p 20 © Jupiterimages, p 21 © Matrishva Vyas, © Evelyn D. Harrison, p 22 © Nobby Clarke, © frank60, © Evelyn D. Harrison, © Claudio Bertoloni, p 24 © Joan Peno McCool

24